FLORAL
Interpretations for Silk Ribbon

FLORAL
Interpretations for Silk Ribbon

HELEN DAFTER

SALLYMILNER
PUBLISHING

First published in 2007 by
Sally Milner Publishing Pty Ltd
734 Woodville Road
Binda NSW 2583 Australia

© Helen Dafter 2007

Design: Anna Warren, Warren Ventures Pty Ltd
Editing: Anne Savage
Artwork: Naomi Dafter
Photography: Tim Connolly

Printed in China

National Library of Australia Cataloguing-in-Publication data:

Dafter, Helen.
 Floral interpretations for silk ribbon.

ISBN 9781863513739 (pbk.).

1. Ribbon flowers. 2. Silk ribbon embroidery. I. Title.
(Series : Milner craft series).

746.447

Disclaimer
Information and instructions given in this book are presented in good faith, but no warranty is given nor results guaranteed, nor is freedom from any patent to be inferred. As we have no control over physical conditions surrounding application of information herein contained in this book, the author and publisher disclaim any liability for untoward results.

10 9 8 7 6 5 4 3 2 1

Dedication

This book is dedicated to the memory of Edna Irene Demsey,
a very strong and gracious lady who introduced me to the world of flowers.
I never walk past a gardenia without thinking of you.

For embroidery project details for the gardenia see page 68.

CONTENTS

THE PROJECTS

Acknowledgements

Putting this book together has given me enormous pleasure. I would once again like to thank my publishers for the creative opportunity of writing and embroidering. It has been an exercise of sheer indulgence satisfying two personal pleasures—my love of flowers, and the enjoyment I get stitching and creating embroideries with silk ribbon.

During the course of my work over the last six years, with the extensive travel involved, I have had the occasional opportunity to indulge in another hobby—photography, most often of flowers and gardens.

In the research and selection process for the flowers in this book I have been able to revisit many places through my extensive library of digital photographs and recall many happy memories of time spent enjoying the labours of fellow flower and garden enthusiasts. My sincere thanks to the gardeners involved in this project, most often without their knowledge. It was the results of their labour that sowed the seed of an idea. The photographs have been the inspiration behind the projects in this book. Where possible, and often with the use of considerable artistic licence, I have used them to create the projects.

Public, private and commercial gardens, and some of the most unlikely places, were subjected to my camera lens and then ultimately interpreted with my needle and silk ribbon. The daffodils were found by the hundred at the edge of a country road bordering a sheep paddock—opportunities for embroidery compositions can be found in the most unlikely places.

Designing and stitching the projects has been both challenging and rewarding. The flowers selected have meant that in some cases I needed to increase the combinations of stitches used to create them. Others remain very simple embroideries with basic stitches used in effective ways. I hope you enjoy them and gain as much inspiration and pleasure from them as I have.

I wish to thank once again my family, my husband Glenn, but most especially my daughter Naomi, a talented and very gifted graphic designer and illustrator. She has painted the delicate watercolours used throughout the book. They may prove useful to you.

HELEN DAFTER

INTRODUCTION

The ribbon embroideries and flower studies from ribbon featured in this book have been based on photographs. Delicate watercolour studies of each of the flowers have also been produced. Some of these are quite detailed and others just a background or wash effect.

The photographs and watercolours are included for your enjoyment and benefit. With the use of a scanner and colour printer you may like to transfer the watercolour of any chosen flower to the fabric of your choice to use as a background for your embroidery. This will create a 'print' to be embellished with silk ribbons and threads. With each watercolour study I have included a detailed drawing of the stitches recommended to complete the embroidery design.

Commercial printers can also complete this scanning and printing process. Your local colour copy shop should have the facilities to do this for you. Please keep in mind the copyright implications—these watercolours have been included for your personal use only.

You may choose, as I have, to interpret the flowers directly onto fabric, perhaps even duplicating and combining them to create or enlarge a design.

Flowers from the photographs have in some instances been adapted in position or in overall composition to enable a simpler embroidery to be completed. Creative silk ribbon embroidery such as these projects allows you to combine, delete, embellish and enlarge to whatever scale or size is required. The only restriction is the size of the ribbon you choose to work with.

Happy stitching!

Silk ribbons

Silk embroidery ribbon is specifically designed and manufactured to be drawn through fabric using only a needle. It has woven edges but these are invisible. Ribbon is available in five different widths—2 mm, 4 mm, 7 mm, 13 mm and 32 mm. Approximately 185 plain dyed colours are available in the most commonly used width, 4 mm. The other four widths are not available in the same extensive colour range.

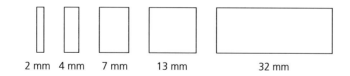

2 mm 4 mm 7 mm 13 mm 32 mm

Specialty hand-dyed silk ribbon is becoming increasingly available. The colour of these ribbons varies along their length, shading from light to dark, and often with different complementary colours appearing as well. These hand-dyed ribbons are usually created by talented cottage industry artists and have good colour repeatability. A word of warning—the quantity of ribbon required for any project using hand-dyed ribbon should be purchased all at the one time as there may be subtle differences from one dye lot to the next. I find the wider hand-dyed ribbons, in particular the 7 mm ones, particularly useful as their changing tones and colours can bring an embroidery to life very quickly, delicately echoing the changing tones of flower petals and leaves.

Other types and widths of ribbon may be used for ribbon embroidery, with various effects achieved with the different materials. Two in particular are worthy of special mention.

Spark organdie A sheer organza ribbon, available once again in different widths, and very useful for subtle filling of background areas. It has an inherent sparkle which can be useful to lift areas of a design as well.

Hanah silk A bias width of silk fabric cut with a hot knife to ribbon width—9 mm, 16 mm, 25 mm and wider. It is hand-dyed. Due to the bias cutting this 'ribbon' frays easily when drawn through fabric but can give very interesting and dimensional effects when used in conjunction with more traditional silk ribbon embroidery techniques. Hanah silk can be used to create larger and more three-dimensional hand-formed flowers that can be sewn onto the surface of fabric rather than through it, as with traditional stitching. The term I use for this type of work is 'hand formed and sculpted flowers'.

Ironing the ribbon

A newly purchased length of silk ribbon often needs to be ironed to remove creases and folds. Ironing will not damage it. The easiest method is to heat the iron, place the ribbon across a flat padded surface, ideally an ironing board, lower the sole of the iron-onto the ribbon and quickly pull the length of ribbon under the iron. After pressing, the ribbon should be stored in such a manner that creases do not reoccur. Winding it around a ribbon storage spool is the best method of storage.

Working length

The ideal length to cut when working with silk ribbon is 30 cm (12 in). Ribbon cut to this length will remain in good condition while you are working it; with a greater length you run the risk of wasting part of it due to ribbon fatigue, caused by being pulled back and forth through the fabric too many times. When working with Hanah silk it can often be an advantage to work with even shorter lengths to further minimise ribbon distress due to the width of this 'ribbon'.

Sewing aids and accessories

Needles

The correct selection of size and type of needle used for silk ribbon embroidery is critical. With the right selection the ribbon will be drawn through the fabric easily and the edges will be protected. If you use the wrong size and type of needle, the ribbon will be difficult to draw through the fabric and the edges will become frayed and distressed, because the ribbon is suffering 'ribbon fatigue'.

The correct size and type of needle will force the fibres of whatever fabric you are working on far enough apart to allow the silk ribbon to be drawn through easily with minimum stress. Silk ribbon is strong, but it is also delicate and needs to be treated with respect.

Needle sizes are based on wire gauge size—the smaller the number the larger the needle.

Size 18 chenille This needle has a large eye, broad shaft and a sharp point, and is the needle most commonly used. It is used for 4 mm and 7 mm silk ribbons and for a broad range of finely woven/knitted fabrics such as silk, cotton and velvet.

Size 20/22 chenille This needle is smaller than the 18 but has the same attributes. It is useful for narrower 2 mm ribbon widths on the closely woven fabrics suggested above, or for use with 4 mm ribbons on more open-weave fabrics such as even-weave fabrics, linen, wool blanketing or wool doctor flannel, where the fibres of the fabric do not need to be pushed as far apart to allow easy passage of the silk.

Size 13 chenille A very large needle but indispensable when working with Hanah silk or some of the wider widths of silk ribbon.

Crewel 8 or 9 This is a general purpose hand-sewing needle with an elongated eye and a sharp point which I prefer when using stranded threads for detail stitching.

Note Needles are the embroiderer's most important 'hand tool'. With constant use or abuse they may become quite blunt. If a chenille needle, which normally has a sharp point, becomes blunt due to accidental damage or extended use, retire it and replace it with a new one. Alternatively, you can try sharpening it using a needle emery. Continued use of a blunt needle will result in ribbon fatigue and wastage.

Embroidery scissors

Always keep a very sharp pair of fine-pointed embroidery scissors close at hand as you work. Use them only for cutting your stranded threads and silk ribbons to length. Never use them for paper or other materials as this will damage the blades and make it difficult to cut cleanly through ribbons and threads.

Fine-tipped water-erasable marking pen

A fine-tipped water-erasable pen is essential for marking designs on your fabric. Any marks visible when the embroidery is complete can be removed by gently dabbing them with a cotton bud (Q-tip) that has been dipped in cold water, then allowing the fabric and ribbon to air dry. Some pens have quite thick tips, and the marks they make can be more difficult to remove. If you are in any doubt that the marks from the pen you intend to use may not be easily removed from the fabric you are

working with, make a test mark on the edge or selvedge of the fabric and try removing it before marking out the entire design.

If you need to mark a design onto a dark fabric use a silver quilting pencil or soft white pencil. The marks they make are not as durable as the marks made by the water-erasable pen, but if you have used the tulle transfer method (see page 23) to mark the design you can always replace the tulle over the design to remark the lines.

Embroidery hoop

A quality embroidery hoop which is easy to adjust and maintains tight even tension is essential. If the correct tension is kept on the fabric you are then free to concentrate on the tension and formation of your stitches and the fabric will not buckle, pull or crease as the stitches are formed. If possible, choose an embroidery hoop that will encompass the outer boundary of your embroidery surface. This will minimise 'bruising' or damaging completed stitches.

My preference is for the Susan Bates Super Grip Lip Hoop. The unique design of this plastic hoop maintains even tension on the fabric and eliminates the need to keep tugging the fabric to keep it taught. It is extremely lightweight and does not cause any wrist strain. If you are working on a square piece of fabric in a round embroidery hoop, use four safety pins in the corners of the fabric to pin the excess safely out of the way. This will eliminate the risk of the excess fabric accidentally being sewn to the back of the work.

A 20 cm (8 in) embroidery hoop is an ideal size and my personal favourite to work with. If you are working on a smaller piece of precious fabric and only have a hoop of this size, strips of calico or cotton fabric can be sewn to the edges of the embroidery fabric so that it will 'fit' the hoop.

Pin/needle cushion

A pin/needle cushion kept close to where you are working is invaluable when working with silk ribbon. Mine holds a collection of chenille needles and crewel needles which are still threaded with the colours I have used on previous projects. By leaving the ribbon attached to the needle (see Locking On, under Getting Started) and using up the leftover ribbon prior to cutting a new length in the same colour I avoid wasting ribbon and get the maximum stitching from each length.

Iron-on interfacing

A soft and flexible iron-on interfacing is a useful aid for making silk ribbon embroidery a little easier. I use it on all fabrics except wool blanketing or wool doctor flannel. The interfacing performs three tasks. Firstly, it stabilises a knitted fabric such as panne velvet, minimising the stretch and making it easier to embroider through. Secondly, it decreases the opacity of a light-coloured fabric—dark ribbons and threads are more difficult to see through the fabric, making it possible to jump short distances with less danger of 'shadowing' showing through to the front of the work. Thirdly, it allows you to bury the ends of the ribbon between the two layers of fabric to end off without having to secure the ends (see further note on Finishing Off). This is the greatest bonus of using interfacing, in that all the untidy ends left dangling as you change ribbons are buried between the layers, with the result that there is less opportunity to pull on them as you draw the needle through the fabric and thus damaging surface stitching.

Stranded threads

Stranded threads of some type are usually necessary to complete a silk ribbon project. These are many and varied and personal preference will determine which is used.

For many years now I have preferred to work with Rajmahal stranded art silk, which I have found to be very sympathetic with silk ribbon. The scale of the work will determine how many strands are used but most work is done with either one or two strands. Increase the number of threads used together if a thicker stem is required or change to a thicker thread such as a hand-dyed silk thread similar to a 'broder' cotton. The size 8 or 9 crewel needle is used for these threads. Use the thread in short lengths only, approximately 50 cm (20 in), to minimise thread distress. In some circumstances a combination of stitches with stranded thread for stems will achieve the look required. For example, laying down two or more rows of stem stitch close together and then 'whipping' the stem stitches together will give a more 'rounded' stem.

Fabric selection

The fabrics chosen for the projects in this book are many and varied. I particularly like to work with hand-painted backgrounds or hand-dyed fabrics as they bring the embroidery to life very quickly in a similar fashion to working with hand-dyed silk ribbons. The variations in tones and colours create very realistic flowers with interesting backgrounds.

When you are shopping for interesting and suitable fabrics to use as your embroidery background, consider some of the hand-dyed cotton fabrics primarily produced for the patchwork market. Some of these fabrics are produced with beautiful shading and a sense of movement which can imitate a natural background and in many cases reduce the need for a hand-painted background. Sumptuous fabrics such as silk velvet and silk habutae are also available hand-dyed from specialty suppliers. The combination of hand-dyed fabrics and silk ribbons is an elegant one.

The ease with which the needle size necessary to

protect the ribbon as it is drawn through the fabric is the final determination of the suitability of a fabric.

Most of the woven fabrics available—silk, velvet, cotton, taffeta, silk velvet—are suitable. In fact if the size 18 needle can be drawn through the fabric quite easily then it can be used for silk ribbon embroidery. Obviously some fabrics are easier to use than others. Natural woven fibres such as cotton, wool and silk are easy to work on, as are some polyester/cotton woven blends. Fibres such as polyesters, knitted cotton and panne velvet are a little more challenging to embroider. If they are to be used for silk ribbon embroidery then the use of an iron-on woven interfacing will make these fibres much easier to work with as the interfacing will stabilise the fabric and reduce the amount of 'stretch'.

Painted background treatments

Painted cotton or silk backgrounds can increase the amount of perspective a piece displays. Simple one-colour backgrounds can increase the amount of depth and visual interest of any embroidery. This painting preparation is often an optional touch but it does give you an opportunity to create a sense of perspective before threading a needle.

Below are a number of helpful hints which you should keep in mind when pre-painting fabric for embroidery.

1   *If possible, always work on dry unwashed fabric.*

2   *Many fabrics are suitable to 'paint' but there are subtle differences between them. Cotton such as natural homespun is a personal favourite and probably the easiest to use.*

3   *Acrylic fabric paint is used to create the background for the designs. (If this is difficult to obtain you can use folk art paint mixed with a textile medium.)*

4   *If the item you are pre-painting is designed for use and will need washing, check whether the paint you are using needs to be ironed to 'set' it. Always follow the manufacturer's instructions.*

5   *Inexpensive bristle brushes are effective for applying the paint, as are small soft sea sponges.*

6   *Before application, always dilute the paint to the lightest shade you require. More paint can always be added to increase depth of colour, but paint is almost impossible to remove if applied too heavily in the first instance. A ratio of 1 part paint to 9 parts water (at the most 2 parts paint to 8 parts water) is recommended to start with. When this has been applied to the fabric, stronger highlights of the same colour or a darker shade can be added by applying a little more to the areas where it is required.*

7   *A scrap of the fabric you intend to use is always handy to have close at hand so that you can try the shade before applying it to the working fabric.*

8   *A hair-dryer is a handy tool during the painting process as it can be used to speed up the drying time, particularly between the application of different colours. It can also be useful to spot dry areas where too much water has been applied.*

9   *Always dry a completed area before applying another colour to minimise bleeding.*

10 *If you do happen to apply an area of colour in a deeper shade than you would have liked to begin with, don't try to remove it or water it down—you will just make a mess. Finish the remainder of the painted background and later on you can embroider over the mistake to camouflage it. Chances are any small mistakes in the background can be covered with ribbon embroidery (it is very forgiving) and you will be the only one who knows. You can also disguise small areas where one colour has bled into another by strategically placing suitable flowers over the questionable spots.*

11 *Always keep in mind that you are simply creating a background to embroider over. The painted background does not need to be complicated or a dominant feature. It will become an integral part of the work but not the most important part—that should always be the hand embroidery.*

GENERAL TECHNIQUES

Getting started

Locking on

The technique of 'locking on' will prevent the silk ribbon falling out of the large eye of the chenille needle while you are working. It also allows you to work as much as possible of the cut length of the ribbon—only the last 5 cm (2 in) will be lost. Remember to cut only a 30 cm (12 in) length to minimise ribbon fatigue.

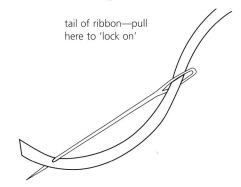

tail of ribbon—pull here to 'lock on'

To lock the ribbon onto the needle, pass the end of the ribbon through the eye of the needle. Bring the threaded end of the ribbon up to the point of the needle and pierce the ribbon approximately 6 mm (¼ in) from the end. Pull this pierced end of the ribbon only halfway down the shaft of the needle. Hold the point of the needle between your thumb and forefinger and gently pull the other end of the ribbon (the tail) to complete the 'locking'.

Soft or loop knot

A quick and effective way to start working with a length of silk ribbon is to create a soft knot or loop which keeps the end of the silk ribbon at the back of the work. The loop so created lies quite flat against the back of the fabric without the bulk of a traditional knot.

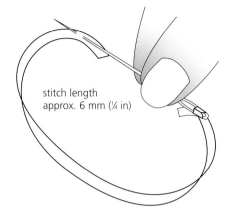

stitch length
approx. 6 mm (¼ in)

Lock the ribbon onto the chenille needle as described above. Hold the long end of the ribbon (the tail) between your thumb and forefinger with the length of ribbon draped away from you over your fingers. Pierce the end of the ribbon twice just above your thumb, approximately 6 mm (¼ in) apart with the point of the needle. This 6 mm stitch should be about 6–8 mm (⅜ in) from the end of the ribbon tail. Grasp the point of the needle and gently pull the needle through the ribbon where you have created this stitch. As you pull this through to the end of the ribbon a 'loop' will be created in the end of the ribbon which will form the 'soft knot'.

A small neat knot at the end of each length of stranded thread is fine for starting—the small lump created will be minimal at the back of the work once silk ribbon is added.

Finishing off

How silk ribbon embroidery is finished off at the back of the work depends on what fabric you are working on, and on the ultimate use of the project. If the embroidery is going to be mounted and framed, it is not as important to finish things off as securely and neatly as it would be if it were a cushion, a blanket or some other item of heavy wear.

Often running the silk ribbon between the surface fabric and the iron-on interfacing is sufficient to hold the end of the ribbon in place until framed or mounted. Never attempt to tie a knot in the end of the silk ribbon you are finishing as this will invariably result in pulled stitches.

Pattern transfer methods

Patterns can be transferred to your chosen embroidery fabric in a variety of ways.

Freehand transfer

This the simplest method, provided you have the confidence and do not mind that not all the design elements will be in the exact position shown on the design outline. Simply draw lines on the fabric using a water-erasable pen, and begin stitching.

Simple transfer method

If the fabric is quite sheer and pale in colour, then quite often it is sufficient to place the design sheet beneath the fabric and simply trace over the major design elements only using a water-erasable pen.

If you have difficulty seeing through the fabric, you can tape pattern and fabric together to a sunlit window, a computer screen, a glass-topped table with a strategic light source beneath it, or to a specially designed light-box, to make the pattern easier to see and trace.

Tulle transfer method

If your chosen embroidery fabric is too thick to see through using one of the methods described above, you may have to employ the tulle transfer method to accurately transfer the elements required.

Place a piece of non-waxed kitchen paper (lunch wrap) or tissue paper over your design sheet. Next, place a piece of fine bridal tulle or netting (available in fabric stores) over the tissue, and pin all three layers together to keep them in place. A permanent black fine-tipped laundry marking pen (available at newsagents) is then used to trace over the design elements to transfer the desired pattern to the tulle. You may not need to transfer the position of every leaf and petal, just the centre position of the flowers and angled lines to represent the stems. This can make the design easier to transfer and interpret. You can always refer back to the original pattern to check precise positions.

Allow the pen marks to dry for several minutes. Remove the pins and discard the paper (which was only there to protect the original pattern sheet). Set the original pattern sheet aside.

Pin the tulle securely to your embroidery fabric

and use a water-erasable fabric marking pen to trace over the lines made by the laundry marker. The fine holes in the tulle allow the tip of the marking pen to penetrate and thus mark the design elements onto your embroidery fabric.

The tulle transfer method is also very useful on dark fabrics which will not allow light to penetrate. A white pencil or a silver quilting pencil may be used to penetrate the tulle on dark-coloured fabrics. Once again, I recommend that you do not try to transfer every detail, just the major design elements. You can otherwise end up with so many lines that it is easy to become confused.

The piece of tulle is now permanently marked with the design, so you will be able to use it again, or perhaps use portions of the design on another project. You can also reverse the design by turning the tulle over.

STITCH GLOSSARY

Many of the stitches used with silk ribbon are traditional embroidery stitches. The one difference is ribbon stitch and its subtle variations.

The following is a comprehensive guide to the stranded thread and silk ribbon stitches I use to create simple and effective designs.

Stem stitch

This stitch is most often worked with stranded thread to create the stems and branches of the various flowers in a design.

Bring the needle up at A, reinsert at B and emerge at C. Repeat the process until the stem is the desired length and shape.

French knot

Often used with silk ribbon to create the centres of flowers or stitched in a group to create flower heads. Occasionally French knots in stranded thread may be used to add additional detail to a flower petal.

Draw the ribbon through the fabric from the back. With the needle point facing away from the fabric, wrap the silk around the needle once only. Stand the needle upright and put the point back into the fabric close to, but not in the same hole, where it emerged. Before pulling the needle and the ribbon through to the back of the fabric pull the ribbon gently but quite firmly around the shaft of the needle and ensure it sits close to the fabric. Pull the needle through to the back of the work. Proceed to the position of the next French knot required or fasten off.

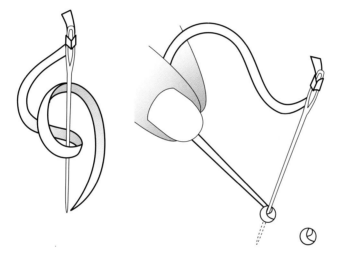

Ribbon stitch

The most commonly used stitch in ribbon embroidery, useful for creating petals, leaves and buds. There are several variations of this stitch.

Draw the ribbon through the fabric at the base of the stitch. Use the shaft of the needle as a tool at the base of the stitch, working it underneath the ribbon to encourage the ribbon to lie as flat as possible on the surface of the fabric. Put the point of the needle through the flattened ribbon 8–10 mm (⅜ in) from the start of the stitch and gently pull the ribbon back on itself until it forms a gentle petal-like point.

This stitch can be angled to the left or right by piercing the ribbon close to its left or right side, but most often is worked straight with the needle piercing the middle of the ribbon.

Extended ribbon stitch

Often worked in conjunction with basic ribbon stitch to create strap-like leaves and grasses. Commence the stitch in the same manner as ribbon stitch, determine the length required, then complete in the same manner as ribbon stitch.

Extended and couched ribbon stitch

Used in a similar way as extended ribbon stitch, this variation has the added advantage of imitating strap-like foliage and leaves that bend over.

Commence the stitch in the same manner as for basic ribbon stitch, determine the length required to the fold line and hold the ribbon flat against the fabric. Take two or three small stitches in a complementary coloured stranded thread across the width of the ribbon to 'couch' it in place on the surface of the fabric. Fold the ribbon over the stranded thread stitches to conceal them and then complete as detailed above.

Twisted ribbon stitch

A useful and easy stitch which allows you to create more interesting leaves and grasses. It is formed in the same way as traditional ribbon stitch, but the ribbon is allowed to twist one or more times before completing the stitch

Straight stitch

This stitch can be worked in either stranded thread or silk ribbon. Using stranded thread, straight stitch is useful to create detail stitching on a flower petal, such as the face of a pansy, or the veins on a leaf. Worked in silk ribbon, straight stitch is often used to create leaves and add interest to backgrounds.

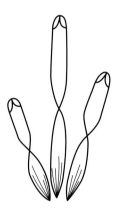

Spider web woven rose

An easy technique combining two types of stitch that creates a realistic open rose. Using two strands of thread in the same colour as the ribbon chosen for the rose, begin with a double knot and work the foundation stitches of the rose using five even length and evenly spaced straight stitches. Anchor this thread off at the back of the work with a double knot. Draw the length of ribbon through the fabric close to the centre of one of the segments, and turn the needle several times until there are several twists in the ribbon. Reverse the needle and simply weave the eye of the needle with the ribbon attached under and over the spokes alternately. The first round should be pulled quite tight. Allow each subsequent round of woven ribbon to sit next to the one before it. Avoid pulling the ribbon too tightly on subsequent rounds as you weave the ribbon, as this will create a bulky rose and waste ribbon. If you have twisted the ribbon sufficiently the twists will form natural-looking petals as you weave. Return the ribbon to the back of the fabric once all the spokes are hidden, and fasten off.

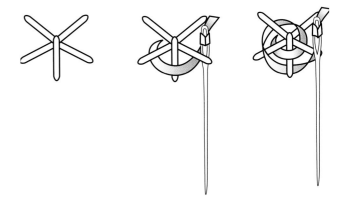

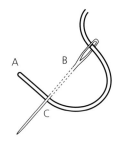

Fly stitch

This useful stitch is most commonly worked with stranded thread, and is often used for creating the detail stitching around a ribbon stitch to create a bud.

Draw the thread through fabric at A, insert at B and emerge at C, insert the needle through to the back of the fabric at D, the required distance below C.

Bullion detached chain stitch

This stitch creates attractive buds and leaves or petals with a fine directional point and is very useful for creating native flowers, and the buds of flowers such as daffodils and roses.

Draw the ribbon through the fabric. Reinsert the needle next to the starting point but not in the same hole, then bring the point of the needle out at the length you want the stitch to be, usually 10–12 mm (⅜–½ in). Before pulling the needle through the fabric, wrap the silk ribbon once around the point of the needle, ensuring that it lies flat, with no creases around the shaft. Keep the tension on the ribbon at the base of the stitch with your thumb or

finger tip, and gently pull the remainder of the needle shaft through the fabric and then the wrap of silk.

Lay the stitch on the fabric, determine which way it will lie best and then take the needle through the fabric immediately above the top edge of the wrap, taking care to angle the stitch in the desired direction.

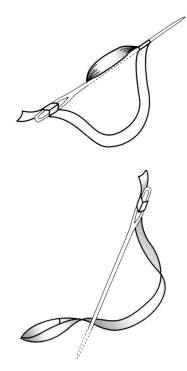

Gathered French knot flower

An extremely useful stitch which can be worked in a variety of ribbon widths to great effect in creating flower clusters or single flowers.

Draw the ribbon through the fabric, follow the directions for the formation of a French knot wrap around the needle above but ensure that the knot is firmly wrapped around the shaft of the needle approximately 2.5 cm (1 in) from the fabric surface. Pull the point of the needle back until it is just below the wrap of ribbon around the needle. Weave the point of the needle in and out of the 2.5 cm (1 in) of ribbon between the wrap on the needle and the fabric surface—you should be able to take the needle in and out five or six times. Take the needle through the fabric next to where it came up and pull it through to the back. The gathers of ribbon will sit on the surface of the fabric with a neat French knot sitting in the middle.

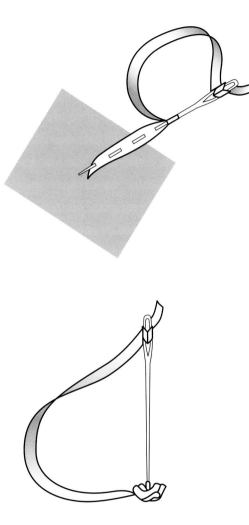

31

Full-blown cabbage rose

This ribbon flower is created with a specific number of stitches sewn in a predetermined order.

The rose requires 11 stitches to complete. Following the diagram, work stitches 1 to 8 around a small oval space as shown. Stitches 1 to 6 are the same length, stitches 7 and 8 are shorter. Stitches 9 to 11 are worked in the order shown through the small oval left empty in the middle of petals 1 to 8. These last three stitches form the outer petals of the rose.

Loop stitch

Used to create dimensional petals or flower trumpets, this stitch is another variation of ribbon stitch. Draw the ribbon through the fabric and flatten as much as possible by running the shaft of the needle underneath the ribbon. If you wish to give the stitch more stability, make two or three small couching stitches in a complementary coloured stranded thread to catch the ribbon to the fabric. Loop the ribbon back over these stitches—don't put too much tension on it—and complete the stitch leaving the loop sitting proud of the surface.

Pistil stitch

A remote French knot with a 'tail' between fabric and knot. Using stranded threads this stitch is useful to create stamens and detail stitching in flower centres.

Detached chain stitch (lazy daisy)

Bring ribbon or thread through at A, take needle through the fabric at B, re-emerge at C and draw needle through fabric, ensuring the ribbon or thread is beneath the needle shaft. Take the needle down through the fabric over the thread or ribbon to fasten off. Position A and B as far apart as necessary.

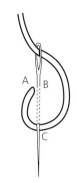

Partly open flower buds: combining stitches

Realistic flower buds can be worked with various combinations of ribbon stitch, fly stitch and straight stitch, as illustrated here. The shape of the particular bud required will dictate which combination you choose.

Pointed flower bud: combining stitches

Long, pointed buds such as those of roses and daffodils are worked with a single bullion detached chain stitch combined with a fly stitch and several straight stitches.

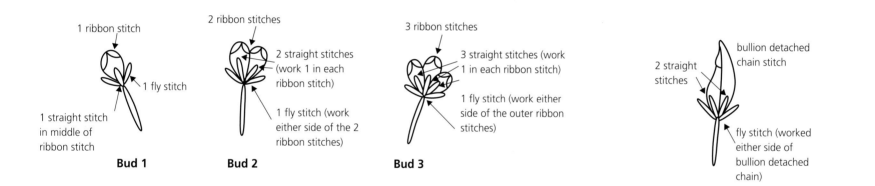

1 ribbon stitch

1 fly stitch

1 straight stitch in middle of ribbon stitch

Bud 1

2 ribbon stitches

2 straight stitches (work 1 in each ribbon stitch)

1 fly stitch (work either side of the 2 ribbon stitches)

Bud 2

3 ribbon stitches

3 straight stitches (work 1 in each ribbon stitch)

1 fly stitch (work either side of the outer ribbon stitches)

Bud 3

2 straight stitches

bullion detached chain stitch

fly stitch (worked either side of bullion detached chain)

HAND-FORMED & SCULPTED FLOWERS

Folded ribbon rose or rosebud

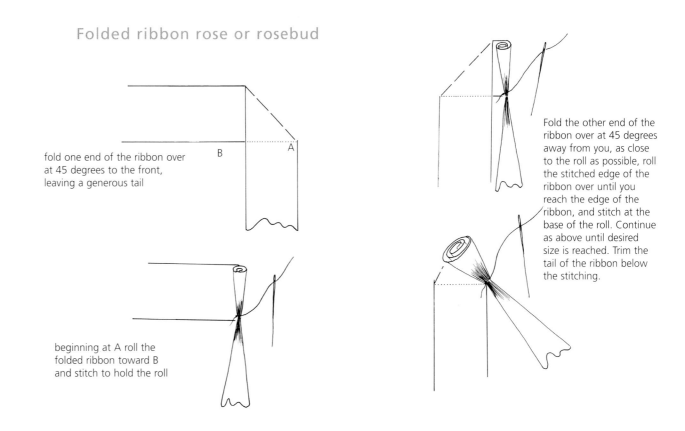

fold one end of the ribbon over at 45 degrees to the front, leaving a generous tail

beginning at A roll the folded ribbon toward B and stitch to hold the roll

Fold the other end of the ribbon over at 45 degrees away from you, as close to the roll as possible, roll the stitched edge of the ribbon over until you reach the edge of the ribbon, and stitch at the base of the roll. Continue as above until desired size is reached. Trim the tail of the ribbon below the stitching.

Gathered flower petal or leaf

gather along three edges with
neat running stitch, pull up to
form each individual petal

individual petal: dot indicates where
top of petal is sewn to fabric

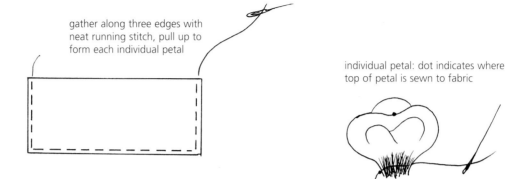

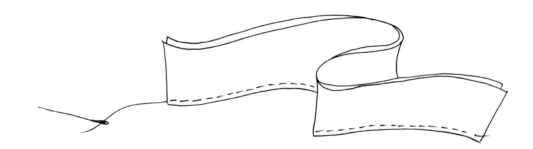

fold the Hanah silk in half, run a neat gathering stitch
along folded edge, draw up gathers and stitch in the
centre of the petals in a meandering fashion

straight stitch

ribbon

stranded
thread

French knot

ribbon

stranded
thread

ribbon stitch

extended ribbon stitch

extended and couched ribbon stitch

twisted ribbon stitch

spider woven rose

bullion detached chain stitch

gathered French knot flower

full blown cabbage rose

fly stitch

loop stitch

pistil stitch

detached chain stitch

flower buds

pointed bud

STITCHING & DESIGN TECHNIQUES

Scale: increasing and decreasing

Creating flowers that are realistic in shape is one thing, creating them to scale is another. The selected ribbon width is going to determine how large a flower is and in that we are restricted with the widths commercially available.

Many of the flowers in these designs have been created smaller than real life. There are exceptions to this. The gardenia is close to actual size, as are the flannel flowers and violas. The camellias, which technically are not embroidered, but hand-formed and sculpted using a variety of techniques and then stitched into place, are also close to their natural size.

The two lavender projects illustrate the effective use of 4 mm silk ribbon for flowers at completely different scales. The embroidery of the lavender border features 4 mm silk ribbon to create the leaves and flower spikes. For the delicate lavender spray, illustrated with a watercolour and a detailed drawing, the silk ribbons suggested are also 4 mm wide.

The daffodil project, because of the small scale of the design, is worked with 2 mm and 4 mm silk ribbons. The same design could just as easily be worked with 4 mm and 7 mm silk ribbons, which would increase the finished size considerably.

If the size of a flower needs to be increased then change to a wider ribbon if at all possible—simply increasing the length of a stitch to make a flower larger will result in distortion and make the flower look odd.

Always consider the required completed size of a design before choosing alternative ribbon widths, and be aware that not all colours are available in all the widths.

Laying out the stitch

'Laying out the stitch' refers to the use of the chenille needle to manipulate the ribbon to keep it as flat as possible during the formation of ribbon stitch. This ensures the ribbon lies at its maximum width at the centre of each stitch. The needle shaft is narrower than the width of the ribbon, thus when the ribbon is drawn through the fabric it will be reduced in width and there will be folds at the edges. Use the shaft of the needle to encourage these folds to be as short as possible and to lie underneath the ribbon when the stitch is completed. If the folds are facing up when the ribbon is pulled through the fabric, twist and turn the ribbon over, then use the needle shaft to gently lay the ribbon in place before piercing the middle of the ribbon to complete the stitch.

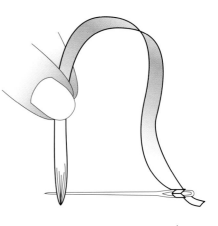

Order of work

In some instances the order in which you do the work in an embroidery is very important to reduce the risk of pulling existing stitches, or to create a dimensional appearance, or both completing those stitches which create the background of the work first and building up 'layers' of stitches as you work.

Always work from the 'back' of the embroidery forward.

Perspective

Once you have mastered the basic stitches for ribbon embroidery it is a very simple matter to adjust the position and length of these stitches to create many varied and interesting looks for the flowers you embroider. This type of stitching is important in creating realistic effects to make flowers look as natural as possible. Flowers rarely face in one direction in nature, so the ability to work them at different angles and emulate their natural growth habits with the use of perspective stitching is an advantage.

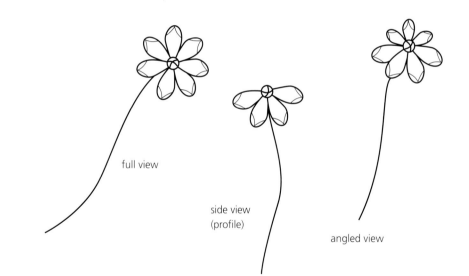

full view

side view
(profile)

angled view

Economical use of silk ribbon

Leaving each piece of silk ribbon attached to a needle until it is completely used up will ensure that there is no wastage of ribbon that has been cut to a working length

Working ribbon embroidery stitches, particularly ribbon stitch itself, in a certain order can make an enormous difference to the amount of ribbon which is visible as stitches on the front of the work and the amount of ribbon 'wasted' in jumping from one stitch to the next at the back of the work. Sensible stitching regimes can achieve this with minimal waste.

To jump or not to jump

A common-sense approach is required when deciding if you are to jump across at the back of the work to the next flower or stitch embroidered with the same coloured ribbon or thread. Ensure there will be no shadowing effect of dark threads or ribbons through to the front of the work. Minimise wastage of ribbon—don't jump if a long loop of ribbon is going to be left at the back of the work as this will invariably result in getting caught on fingers or needles, etc. which will result in damaged stitches. Keep the above in mind as you stitch and 'jump' to achieve neat, tidy and economical stitching.

Perfect petal placement

To achieve evenly spaced petals on simple flowers such as daisies, forget-me-nots and so on comes with practice. Until that skill is acquired keeping a few simple techniques in mind as you stitch will make it easier.

Draw a line to represent the middle of each petal using a water-erasable pen. If the petal is to be created using a simple ribbon stitch this mark only needs to be a straight line to represent the length and position of the stitch required.

To get all the petals the same length try drawing a circle around the flower centre with a coin or use a clear plastic circle template of the required size. The flower centre is in the middle of the circle and then ribbon stitches of even length are laid down around the flower centre extending to the circle drawn on the fabric. Providing the flower centre is in the middle of the circle all the petals will be the same length.

This technique can also be used when creating flowers with perspective—simply offset the flower centre and work petals to the circle edge.

To ensure that the petals are evenly spaced around the circle and the flower centre keep the following in mind.

Flowers with five petals Mark the fabric with a Y, then draw in two more lines to complete the five evenly spaced spokes.

Flowers with six evenly spaced petals Mark the fabric with three intersecting fine lines—from 12 o'clock to 6 o'clock, from 2 o'clock to 8 o'clock, and from 4 o'clock to 10 o'clock.

Flowers with eight evenly spaced petals Mark the fabric with four intersecting fine lines—from 12 o'clock to 6 o'clock, from 1.30 to 7.30, from 3 o'clock to 9 o'clock, and from 4.30 to 10.30.

If more than eight petals are required, generally the flower centre will be created using more than one French knot, most likely a cluster, and the width of the ribbon will determine the number of petals. Simply work the flower petals as evenly as possible, spacing them by eye as you go.

Camouflage or waste stitch

This is one of the most useful stitching techniques to keep in mind as you work, particularly until you get a feel for the correct tension required for the various stitches and understand manipulation of the ribbon to get it to sit flat on the fabric. A camouflage or waste stitch is required if you accidentally 'pull' the end of the ribbon stitch you are creating through to the back of the fabric. Because the formation of a ribbon stitch requires you to pull the ribbon back through itself it is almost impossible to undo—and it leaves a large hole in the ribbon if you do manage to undo it. Rather than cutting the stitch out, having to sew down the cut end near the previous stitch and re-knot your ribbon, it is easier to create a camouflage stitch to disguise the stitch that has been pulled. Simply tension the pulled stitch as much as possible to make the ribbon thinner, and work a perfectly formed ribbon stitch straight over the top of the tensioned one. This will cover the stitch, is less wasteful of ribbon and allows you to move quickly on to the next stitch.

Colour selection

Putting a working combination of colours together for an innovative and creative design is often a confusing and difficult task for embroiderers who are just starting out.

With most projects for this book the colours of the flowers featured in the photographs and the colours of the silk ribbons available have guided me. The exception is the gerberas. I am not fond of orange flowers, although I do appreciate their place in the garden. I looked at the structure of the flowers in the photograph and recreated them with a more personally acceptable range of colours that I had seen in a collection of gerberas at a local florist. The gerberas photographed have been depicted in

the accompanying watercolour for your use. If you are unable to find the exact colour of ribbon for a flower you wish to stitch then choose the closest colour and allow artistic licence to compensate for subtle differences in colour and tone.

The extras

A number of the embroideries feature hand-dyed lace leaves and motifs to complement the flowers created in silk. The lace motifs allow leaves whose size and shape would often be difficult to achieve with silk ribbon to be incorporated in a design. They have also been used to create a more dimensional effect. The leaves have been dyed using a variety of colours or combinations of colours, allowed to dry, often cut apart into smaller individual sections and then stitched into position. Embroidered leaves in some of the wider silk ribbons, 13 mm or hand-formed leaves from Hanah silk may be substituted for the lace motifs if desired.

THE PROJECTS

Lavender

With its nostalgic, old-fashioned associations, lavender is perhaps the easiest flower to interpret with silk ribbon.
Many modern hybrid cultivars have been developed to thrive in a wide variety of growing conditions.
The embroidery of a lavender border is based on the photograph of a 20 metre (65 foot) border in full bloom
taken in New Zealand at St Margaret's Country Garden.
The watercolour spray on page 61, detailed as a black and white line drawing, depicts English lavender,
in my opinion the most fragrant of all.

Requirements

20 x 10 cm (8 x 4 in) hand-dyed silk habutae, Colour
    Streams 'Salt Bush'

20 x 10 cm (8 x 4 in) hand-dyed silk velvet, Colour Streams
    'Salt Bush'

25 cm (10 in) square iron-on interfacing

Rajmahal stranded art silk: 113, 521, 805, 925

Colour Streams silk thread:

2 m x Ophir 'Eucalypt'

2 m x Exotic Lights 'Eucalypt'

4 mm silk ribbons:

    2 m x colours 32, 33, 178, 179

no. 9 crewel needles for use with stranded threads

no. 18 chenille needles for use with silk ribbons

embroidery hoop: a 20 cm (8 in) hoop will allow
    completion of work without repositioning

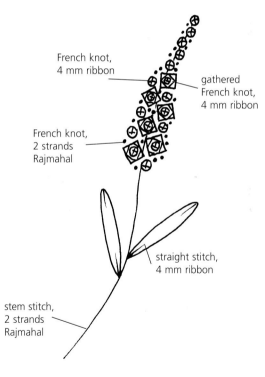

French knot,
4 mm ribbon

gathered
French knot,
4 mm ribbon

French knot,
2 strands
Rajmahal

straight stitch,
4 mm ribbon

stem stitch,
2 strands
Rajmahal

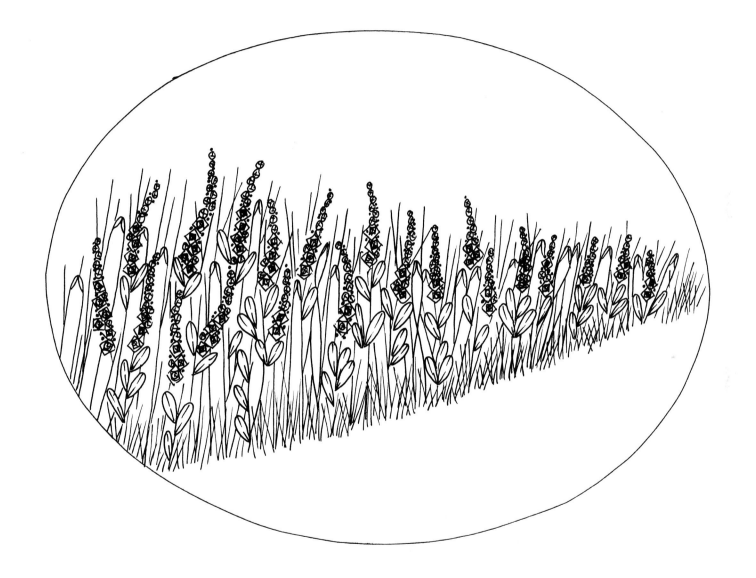

Method

Place the silk habutae and velvet face down on a flat surface, with the long edges butted together. Fuse the iron-on interfacing, as one piece, to the two fabrics with a hot iron. The join between the fabrics, held together with the interfacing only, will later be completely concealed by the embroidery. Transfer the design to the fabric. This may only involve a triangular shape—variations to the placement of grasses, flowers and leaves will not affect the integrity of the design providing it narrows at one end. Fit fabric to embroidery hoop and adjust tension as necessary. Follow the instructions below for the order of work and stitches used to complete the project.

Background grasses: Work a light background of straight stitches in varying lengths and angles across the design in a mixture of Rajmahal 805 and 925, and silk threads Ophir 'Eucalypt' and Exotic Lights 'Eucalypt'.

Foreground grasses: Work straight stitches and ribbon stitches in 4 mm silk ribbon x colour 33 across the design, echoing the angles of the background grasses and filling in any vacant spaces.

Lavender stems: Using the finished embroidery and the design outline as guides, work a number of gently curved stems in stem stitch, 2 strands Rajmahal 805. Note that many of the stems do not need stitching in full as they hide behind grasses and leaves.

Lavender heads: The flowers for each spike are created with 4 mm ribbon in either colour 178 or 179, worked as French knots and gathered French knots. Any visible spaces between the silk ribbons are filled with French knots in 2 strands Rajmahal 113.

Lavender leaves: Angled leaves have been placed among the foliage and stems of the lavender in straight stitches pulled tightly from 4 mm silk ribbon colour 32.

Grass edge: The grassy front of the flower border is worked in short straight stitches in 2 strands

Rajmahal 521. Work these at different angles across the base of the design.

Once all the embroidery is complete remove any visible marks from the water-erasable pen by dabbing gently with a cotton bud dipped in water.

Frame or mount as desired.

Watercolour study

This is one of a number of smaller studies based on the major project embroideries which are intended to inspire you to create an individual work. I have provided a watercolour background and diagram, and suggested the stitches you might use, but it is up to you to vary the size, the colours and the diagram as you might wish.

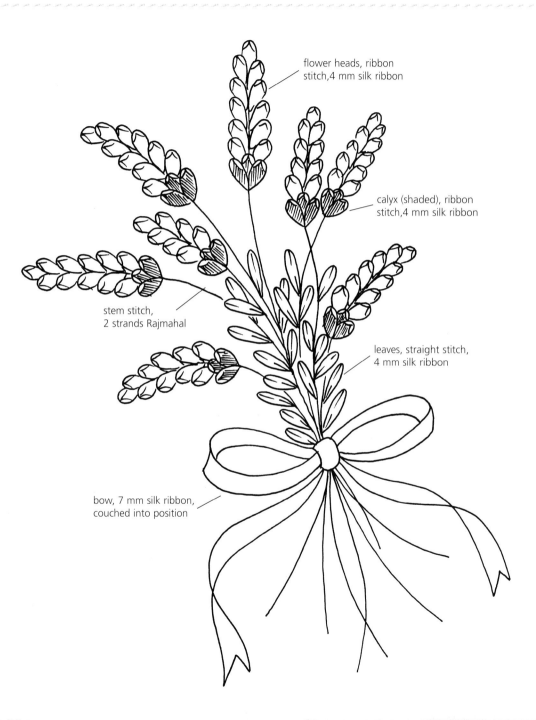

flower heads, ribbon
stitch,4 mm silk ribbon

calyx (shaded), ribbon
stitch,4 mm silk ribbon

stem stitch,
2 strands Rajmahal

leaves, straight stitch,
4 mm silk ribbon

bow, 7 mm silk ribbon,
couched into position

Violas

Of all the members of the viola family that I have seen and photographed, the little bicoloured Johnny-jump-ups remain my favourite. The flowers themselves are quite small but they self-seed easily and a mass grouping of healthy plants in full bloom is stunning. So much reward for very little effort!

4 mm ribbon, ribbon stitch/twisted ribbon stitch

stem stitch, 2 strands Rajmahal

ribbon stitch, 7 mm ribbon

French knot, 4 mm ribbon

straight stitch (dotted lines), 2 strands Rajmahal

straight stitch, 1 strand Rajmahal

The watercolours, two in this case, depict a spray of violas as a possible printed background for the major embroidery, and a lone pansy suitable as a printed background for a card insert or small embroidery.

Requirements

25 cm (10 in) square cotton homespun fabric, cream

20 cm (8 in) square iron-on interfacing

fabric paint, Decoart Americana DA52, if a hand-painted
    background is desired

sea sponge or large bristle brush

(refer to instructions for creating hand-painted
    backgrounds, page 18)

4 mm silk ribbon:
    0.5 m x colour 15
    1 m x colour 72

7 mm silk ribbon:

0.5 m x colour 101

1 m x colour 117

1 m x colour 84

Rajmahal stranded art silk: 29, 93, 521

7 hand-dyed lace leaves, or ribbons to create alternative leaves

no. 9 crewel needle for use with silk threads

no. 18 chenille needle for use with silk ribbons

20 cm (8 in) embroidery hoop allows completion of work without repositioning

Method

Transfer the design to the prepared hand-painted background using a water-erasable pen. Fuse the iron-on interfacing to the back of the fabric. Fit fabric to embroidery hoop and adjust tension as necessary. If you are using the hand-dyed lace leaves, they need to be positioned and stitched into place prior to beginning the embroidery. Some of the embroidery stitches are worked through the leaves to increase the perception of depth.

Follow the instructions below for the order of work, the stitches and colours used to complete the project.

Flower centres: 4 mm silk ribbon x colour 15; 1-wrap French knot

Upper petals: 7 mm silk ribbon x colour 84; ribbon stitch

Middle petals: 7 mm silk ribbon x colour 118; ribbon stitch

Lower petals: 7 mm silk ribbon x colour 101; ribbon stitch

Detail on lower petals: Embroider straight stitches of varying lengths close together on the lower petals only; 2 strands Rajmahal 93.

Detail on middle and lower petals: Embroider straight stitches of varying lengths on the middle petals and over the top of existing straight stitches on lower petals; 1 strand Rajmahal 29.

Stems: Work the gently curving stems of each of the buds; 2 strands Rajmahal 521.

Buds: Work ribbon stitches in 7 mm ribbon in 84 and 117 (refer photograph of project).

Bud calyces: 4 mm silk ribbon x colour 72; ribbon stitch/twisted ribbon stitch as detailed on illustration

Finishing

Once all the embroidery is complete remove any visible marks from the water-erasable pen by dabbing gently with a cotton bud dipped in water.

Frame or mount as desired.

Watercolour study

These two small studies based on the major violas embroidery are intended to inspire you to create an individual work. I have provided a watercolour background and diagram, and suggested the stitches you might use, but it is up to you to vary the size, the colours and the diagram as you might wish.

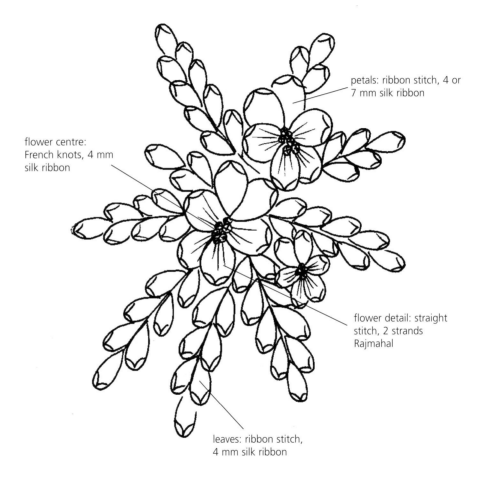

petals: ribbon stitch, 4 or
7 mm silk ribbon

flower centre:
French knots, 4 mm
silk ribbon

flower detail: straight
stitch, 2 strands
Rajmahal

leaves: ribbon stitch,
4 mm silk ribbon

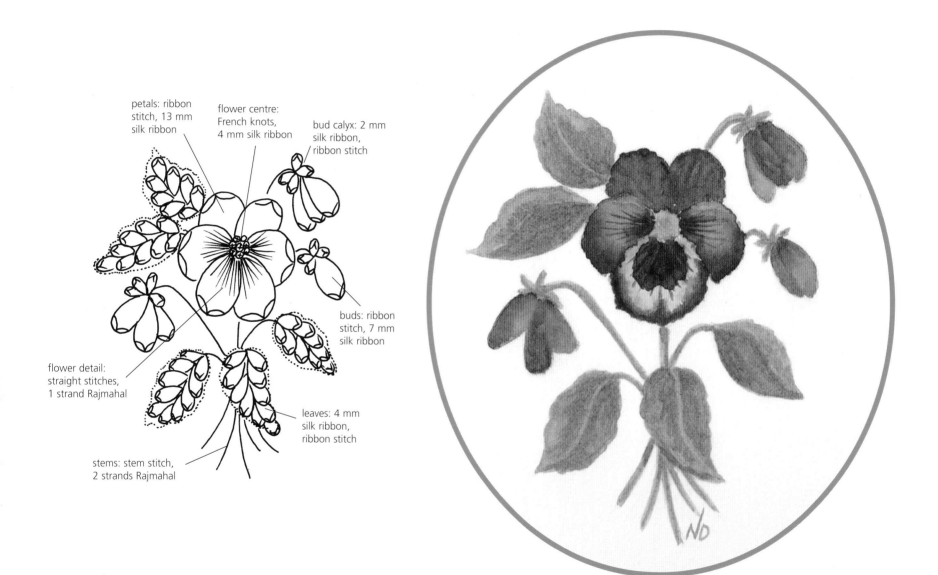

petals: ribbon
stitch, 13 mm
silk ribbon

flower centre:
French knots,
4 mm silk ribbon

bud calyx: 2 mm
silk ribbon,
ribbon stitch

buds: ribbon
stitch, 7 mm
silk ribbon

flower detail:
straight stitches,
1 strand Rajmahal

leaves: 4 mm
silk ribbon,
ribbon stitch

stems: stem stitch,
2 strands Rajmahal

GRAPE HYACINTH

The grape hyacinth is one of my favourite bulbs—the colour is magnificent, although the flowers, as far as bulbs go, are quite unassuming. This photograph was taken very early one morning in the Omaru public gardens. We had the entire place to ourselves and I took many photographs of the spring blooms and thoroughly enjoyed this peaceful and pretty place.

Requirements

20 cm (8 in) square hand-dyed cotton fabric, dark tone
  'Moss'

20 cm (8 in) iron-on interfacing

4 mm silk ribbons:

1 m x colours 20, 21, 72, 75 and 171

3 m Colour Streams 'Jacaranda'

Rajmahal stranded art silk: Ecru, 29, 421, 521

Rajmahal silver hand-sew thread to create the signature
  silver web

1 x size 11 black seed bead for body of spider

no. 9 crewel needle for use with silk threads

no. 18 chenille needle for use with silk ribbons

20 cm (8 in) embroidery hoop allows completion of work
  without repositioning

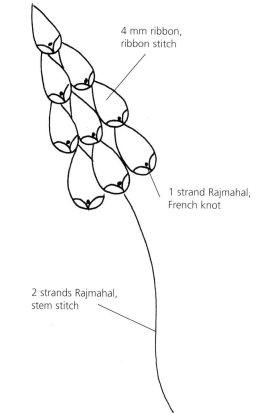

4 mm ribbon,
ribbon stitch

1 strand Rajmahal,
French knot

2 strands Rajmahal,
stem stitch

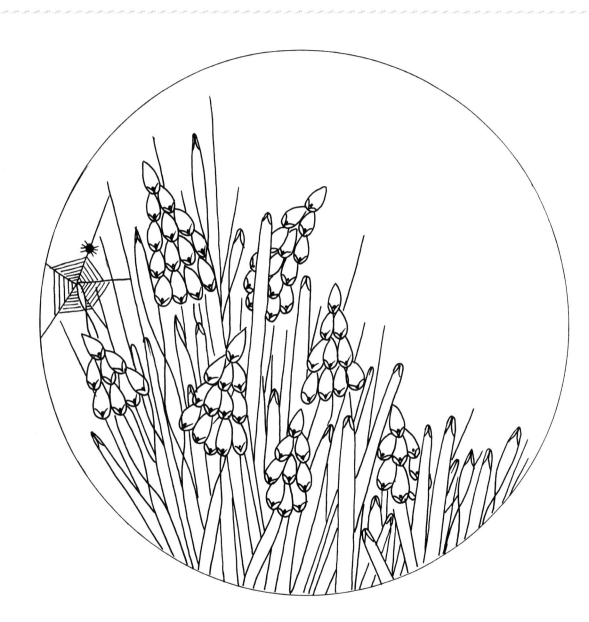

Method

Fuse the interfacing to the back of the cotton fabric. Transfer the design elements required to your fabric (you may need to use the method described for dark fabrics under Pattern Transfer Methods).

The crowded nature of the leaves and grasses depicted at the base of this embroidery mean that you do not have to carefully follow the colours of the various green ribbons used to create them.

Background grasses: Work with 2 strands of Rajmahal in either colour 521 or 421, using long straight stitches worked at different angles and differing lengths across the base of the design.

Reed-like grasses: Using the various colours of 4 mm silk ribbon, complete the thicker reed-like grasses and leaves in straight stitch, ribbon stitch and twisted ribbon stitch.

Flower stems: Worked in 2 strands of Rajmahal thread 521, stem stitch.

Flowers: These are a succession of ribbon stitches worked from the uppermost point of the flower head, increasing or decreasing as illustrated until the flower head is complete. Colour Streams 'Jacaranda' is used for the flowers as the subtle variations of this hand-dyed ribbon echo the true colour of the flower in nature. Delicate French knots using 1 strand of Rajmahal Ecru form the flower detail at the point where the ribbon folds in at the end of each ribbon stitch (see diagram).

Spider web: The silver web is created by stitching 5 evenly spaced but different length spokes to some chosen point in the design using Rajmahal hand-sew silver thread. Individual straight stitches in silver complete each segment of web. Do not take the web stitches over the spokes, as this will distort the spokes.

The tiny spider is created by sewing the bead into position using 4 straight stitches in Rajmahal 29, angled through the bead to create the legs and stitch the bead body onto the fabric at the same time.

A tiny enamelled dragonfly button embellishes one corner of the design.

Once all the embroidery is complete remove any visible marks from the water-erasable pen by dabbing gently with a cotton bud dipped in water. Frame or mount as desired.

Watercolour study

This small study based on the major grape hyacinth embroidery is intended to inspire you to create an individual work. I have provided a watercolour background and diagram, and suggested the stitches you might use, but it is up to you to vary the size, the colours and the diagram as you might wish.

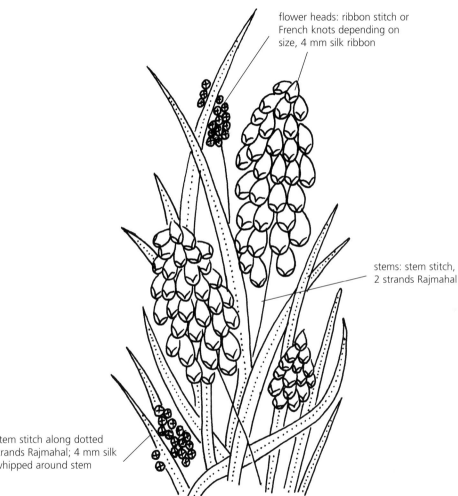

flower heads: ribbon stitch or
French knots depending on
size, 4 mm silk ribbon

stems: stem stitch,
2 strands Rajmahal

leaves: stem stitch along dotted
line, 2 strands Rajmahal; 4 mm silk
ribbon whipped around stem
stitch

GARDENIA

Gardenias will always remain, for sentimental reasons, one of my favourite perfumed flowers. The perfume and the flower, usually a very clear white until it fades with age, are very noticeable, especially at night when the heady fragrance becomes more apparent to our senses. I deliberately kept this project quite small as the top to a lidded box; if a larger project is required simply add more flowers and leaves and perhaps some buds.

Requirements

15 cm (6 in) square hand-dyed cotton fabric, medium
   tone 'Moss'

15 cm (6 in) square iron-on interfacing,

13 mm silk embroidery ribbon, 2 m x colour 3

hand-dyed lace leaves trimmed to suit shapes required

no. 13 chenille needle for use with silk ribbons

15 cm (6 in) embroidery hoop allows completion of work
   without repositioning

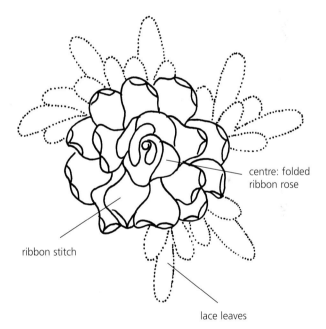

centre: folded
ribbon rose

ribbon stitch

lace leaves

Method

Iron the interfacing to the back of the fabric. Transfer the design to the right side—you will only need to mark the position of the outer leaves as the centre of the flower is formed in the hand and stitched into position after the outer petals of the gardenia are completed.

Outer petals: 13 mm silk ribbon colour 3, ribbon stitch; vary the tension of each stitch and you may also like to vary the position where, across the width of ribbon, the needle point is placed to create each ribbon stitch as this will make each stitch quite distinctive and give the flower its blowsy and unkempt appearance.

Flower centre: Using a length of 13 mm silk ribbon colour 3, and following the instructions for hand-formed rose centres and buds (see Stitch Glossary), complete a flower centre with four or five turns of rolled ribbon only, stitching with toning thread at the base of the flower centre with each turn. Once this is complete, trim the tail of the ribbon close to the holding stitches and, using the same coloured thread, stitch the flower centre in place among the ribbon stitches already completed.

Hand-dyed lace leaves: Trim to fit the edges of the outer petals of the flower, pin and stitch into place using a matching sewing cotton.

Finishing

Once all the embroidery is complete remove any visible marks from the water-erasable pen by dabbing gently with a cotton bud dipped in water.

Frame or mount as desired.

Watercolour study

This small study based is intended to inspire you to create an individual work. I have provided a watercolour background and diagram, and suggested the stitches you might use, but it is up to you to vary the size, the colours and the diagram as you might wish.

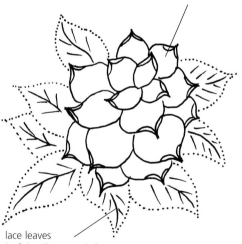

petals: ribbon stitch, 7 mm and 13 mm silk ribbon

lace leaves
leaf detail: stem stitch,
2 strands Rajmahal

DAFFODIL

This photograph, as I mentioned in the introduction, was taken by the side of a country road beneath the fence of a sheep paddock near Te Anau in New Zealand. There was not a house in sight. I have seen daffodils growing in a similar fashion to be enjoyed by all on the outskirts of Kyneton in Victoria. Somebody must have planted them. I hope others enjoy them as much as I do. What tough little characters they must be to survive and indeed thrive and multiply each year in such neglected and harsh conditions.

Requirements

20 cm (8 in) square moiré taffeta

20 cm (8 in) square iron-on interfacing

2 mm silk ribbon: 1 m x colour 15

4 mm silk ribbons:

    1 m x colour 15

    1 m x colour 31

    1.5 m x 32

3 m Glenlorin 'Lillian'

Rajmahal stranded art silk: 805, 926

no. 9 crewel needle for use with silk threads

no. 18 chenille needle for use with silk ribbons

20 cm (8 in) embroidery hoop allows completion of work
   without repositioning

Method

Fuse the interfacing to the back of the taffeta fabric. Transfer the design elements required to your fabric (you may need to use the method described for dark fabrics under Pattern Transfer Methods).

The crowded nature of the leaves and grasses depicted at the base of this embroidery mean that you do not have to carefully match the colours of the green ribbons used to create them.

Background grasses: These are created using 2 strands of Rajmahal, either 805 or 926, using long straight stitches worked at different angles and different lengths across the base of the design.

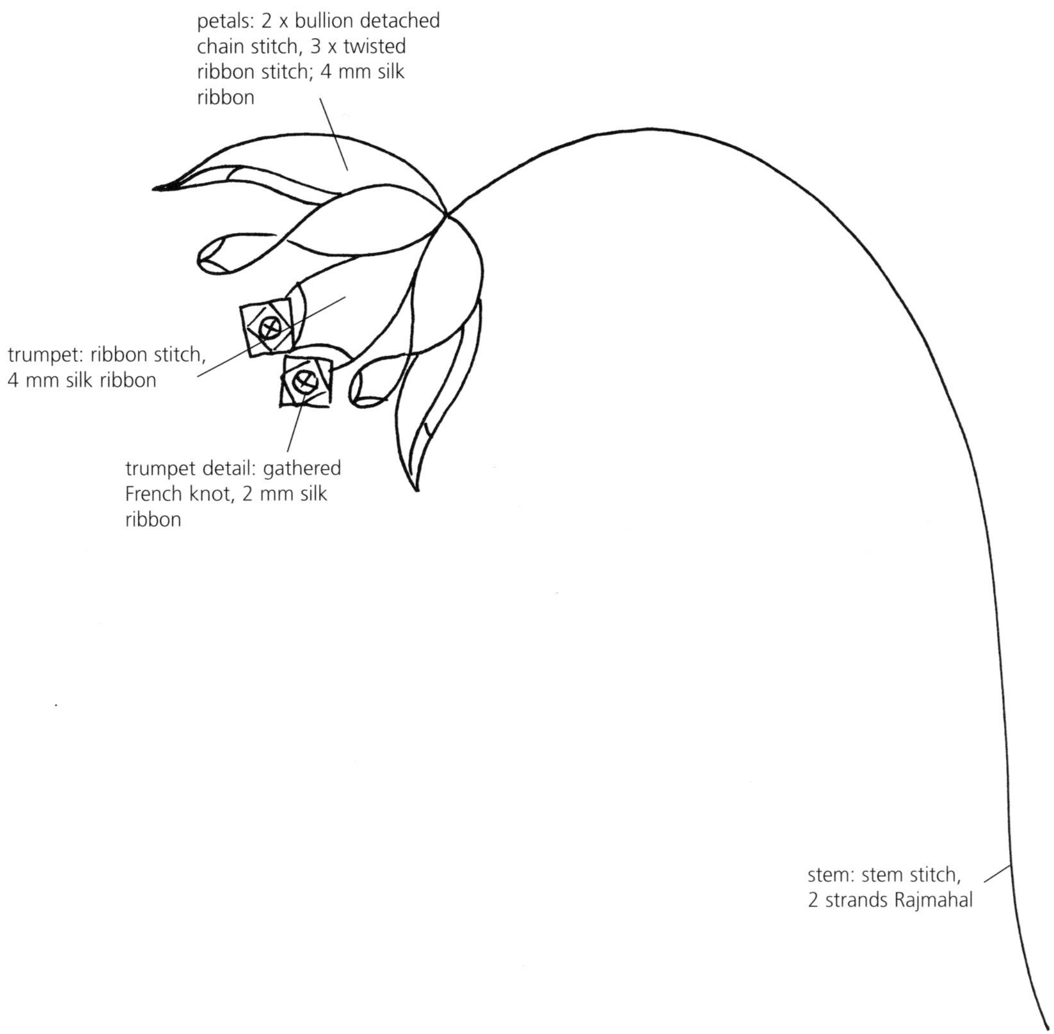

petals: 2 x bullion detached
chain stitch, 3 x twisted
ribbon stitch; 4 mm silk
ribbon

trumpet: ribbon stitch,
4 mm silk ribbon

trumpet detail: gathered
French knot, 2 mm silk
ribbon

stem: stem stitch,
2 strands Rajmahal

In my garden there is
a large place for sentiment.
My garden of flowers is
also my garden of thoughts
and dreams.
The thoughts grow as
freely as the flowers and
the dreams are as beautiful.

Abram L Urban

Daffodil leaves: Using 4 mm silk ribbons 31 and 32, work the thicker daffodil leaves in straight stitch, ribbon stitch and twisted ribbon stitch.

Stems: Work flower stems in 2 strands of Rajmahal 805 in stem stitch.

Daffodil flower: The way the flower is positioned determines whether the petals or the trumpet is stitched first. Refer to diagram and photograph to help determine the order of stitching.

Trumpet: ribbon stitch, 4 mm silk ribbon x colour 15

Trumpet detail: gathered French knot, 2 mm silk ribbon x colour 15

Petals: bullion detached chain stitch or twisted ribbon stitch, 4 mm silk ribbon 'Lillian'

Bud: ribbon stitch, 4 mm silk ribbon x colour 15

Bud calyx: straight stitch, 2 strands Rajmahal 805

A tiny enamelled bee button embellishes one corner of the design.

Finishing

Once all the embroidery is complete remove any visible marks from the water-erasable pen by dabbing gently with a cotton bud dipped in water.

I chose a poem with a gardening theme to enhance the design when it was mounted in the hinged frame.

Watercolour study

This small study based on the major daffodil embroidery is intended to inspire you to create an individual work. I have provided a watercolour background and diagram, and suggested the stitches you might use, but it is up to you to vary the size, the colours and the diagram as you might wish.

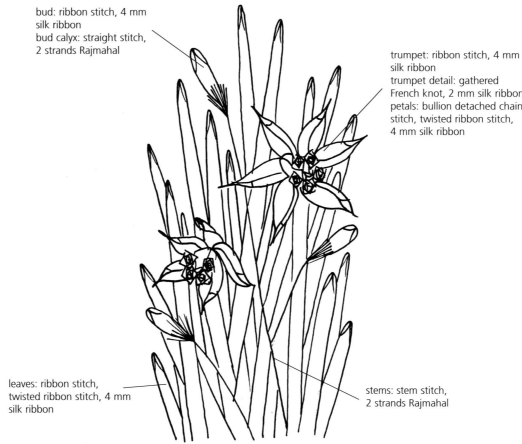

bud: ribbon stitch, 4 mm
silk ribbon
bud calyx: straight stitch,
2 strands Rajmahal

trumpet: ribbon stitch, 4 mm
silk ribbon
trumpet detail: gathered
French knot, 2 mm silk ribbon
petals: bullion detached chain
stitch, twisted ribbon stitch,
4 mm silk ribbon

leaves: ribbon stitch,
twisted ribbon stitch, 4 mm
silk ribbon

stems: stem stitch,
2 strands Rajmahal

Gerbera

The photograph this design was based on featured gerberas in a range of strong orange tones.
I wanted more subtle tones of pink, so I colour-matched ribbons to gerbera flowers found at my local florist.
The reference for the flower shape, petal formation, stems and leaves remained my original photograph.
Once again delicate hand-dyed lace leaves form the gerbera leaves.

Requirements

30 cm (12 in) square dupion silk, light olive green

30 cm (12 in) square iron-on interfacing

Rajmahal stranded art silk: 29, 311, 421, 521

4 mm silk ribbon:

    0.5 m x colour 72

    3 m x colours 5, 8, 112, 114, 128, 129

hand-dyed lace leaves

no. 9 crewel needle for use with silk threads

no. 18 chenille needle for use with silk ribbons

25 cm (10 in) embroidery hoop allows completion of

    work without repositioning

Method

Fuse the interfacing to the back of the dupion silk. Transfer the design elements required to your fabric (you may need to use the method described for dark fabrics under Pattern Transfer Methods).

This design employs stitching methods described under Perspective Stitching, altering the length and position of petals to create flowers depicted at different angles.

Order of work for flower components

Refer to the colour photograph and the chart below for the combination of silk ribbons used to create each flower. The two flowers worked on their side use the same colour combination. The buds are treated separately.

black centre: Rajmahal 29; silk ribbon centre: 8, silk ribbon petals: 5

black centre: Rajmahal 29; silk ribbon centre: 112, silk ribbon petals: 8

gathered French
knots: 4 mm ribbon

French knots:
4 mm ribbon

French knots: 2
strands Rajmahal

loop stitch:
4 mm ribbon

ribbon stitch:
4 mm ribbon

twisted ribbon stitch:
4 mm ribbon

stem stitch: 2 parallel rows x
2 strands Rajmahal whipped
with 2 strands Rajmahal

black centre: Rajmahal 29; silk ribbon centre: 114, silk ribbon petals: 112

black centre: Rajmahal 29; silk ribbon centre: 129, silk ribbon petals: 128

Stems: Work 2 parallel rows of stem stitch close together, using 2 strands Rajmahal, for each flower (colours 311, 421, 521 can be used variably). Then, using 2 strands of one of the other Rajmahal colours, whip the two rows of stem stitch to create a rounded stem for each flower.

Flower centres: Using 2 strands Rajmahal 29, work tight clusters of single-wrap French knots as the centre of each flower. The shape of these centres varies, the three full-face flowers each having a circle, the two flowers in profile having an oval. The ruffled inner centre of each flower is created with a combination of stitches. Gathered French knots in 4 mm silk initially surround the black inner centre circle and are encircled by a row of short loop stitches using the same ribbon.

Outer petals: Finally, petals of uneven lengths are worked around the loop stitches in a paler shade of 4 mm silk (refer to table above and photograph) using ribbon stitch and twisted ribbon stitch to add a little variety and whimsy to the petal formation.

Buds: Work the petals in 4 mm silk ribbon x colour 129, with ribbon stitch and twisted ribbon stitch. The calyx for each bud is worked in short ribbon stitches in 4 mm silk ribbon x colour 72.

Leaves: Stitch the hand-dyed leaves in place at the base of the design. Alternatively, leaves could be worked in a 7 mm ribbon and bullion detached chain stitch.

Finishing

Once all the embroidery is complete remove any visible marks from the water-erasable pen by dabbing gently with a cotton bud dipped in water.

Frame or mount as desired.

flower centres: French knots, 4 mm ribbon

petals: straight stitch, 4 mm ribbon

leaves: outline with stem stitch, 2 strands Rajmahal
vein detail: straight stitch, 2 strands Rajmahal

stems: stem stitch, 2 strands Rajmahal

Watercolour study

This small study based on the major gerbera embroidery is intended to inspire you to create an individual work. I have provided a watercolour background and diagram, and suggested the stitches you might use, but it is up to you to vary the size, the colours and the diagram as you might wish.

Camellia Sasanqua

The background for this project needs to be very muted. A hand-painted wash is all that is required. These flowers are based on the sasanqua camellias in the photograph. Because of the size of the flower, each individual petal was hand-formed and stitched into position, as was the flower's centre. Technically, they are not really embroidered as the ribbon is not taken through the fabric as in traditional ribbon embroidery. Hanah silk is ideal for this type of hand-forming and sculpting, as the widths available will allow the creation of quite large flowers. Hand-dyed lace leaves complete the design.

Requirements

25 cm (10 in) square hand-dyed silk velvet, Colour Streams 'Verde'

25 cm (10 in) square iron-on interfacing

3 m x 25 mm (1 in) Hanah silk ribbon, 'Peaches and Cream'

hand-dyed lace leaf motifs in colour/s complementary to the Hanah silk

coloured sewing thread

no. 9 crewel needle for forming the flower components and stitching them into position

25 cm (10 in) embroidery hoop allows completion of work without repositioning

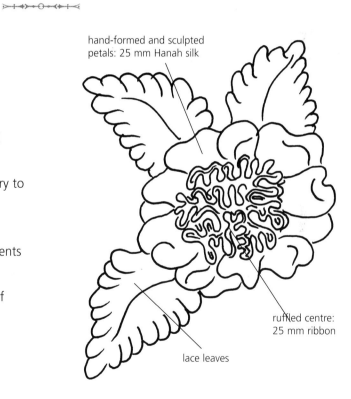

hand-formed and sculpted petals: 25 mm Hanah silk

ruffled centre: 25 mm ribbon

lace leaves

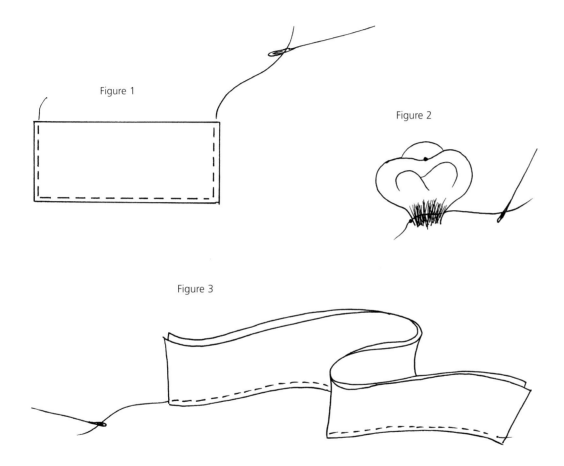

Figure 1

Figure 2

Figure 3

Fuse the interfacing to the back of the silk velvet. Mark the position of the camellias onto the surface of the velvet with a silver quilting pencil—a simple circle will suffice. Each individual petal is stitched into position inside the outer circle, leaving a 1.5 cm (½ in) gap at the centre of the flower. This is filled later with the ruffled ribbon.

Flowers: The larger flower has 12 individual petals and the smaller one 10; you may need more or fewer petals in each case.

To make each petal cut a 6 cm (2¼ in) length of ribbon. Thread the no. 9 crewel needle with complementary coloured sewing thread and knot one end. Using the needle and thread run a small neat gathering stitch around the three sides of the section of ribbon, as shown in Figure 1.

Pull up the gathers gently, as shown in Figure 2, to create a soft loop of ribbon.

Stitch the loop into position so that the top edge of the petal sits just outside the circle marked on the fabric. Continue making petals and stitching into position until the outer edge of the flower is complete. To sculpt the individual petals, bring the thread through from the back of the fabric and take it through the very edge of the petal (marked with a dot on Figure 2), and stitch this into position on the fabric, sculpting the petal edge as you stitch carefully into place.

Centre: Form the ruffled centre of the camellia by cutting a 25 cm (10 in) length of ribbon. Fold this in half lengthways. Using a knotted length of sewing thread, run a gathering stitch along the folded edge of the ribbon as close to the fold as possible. See Figure 3.

When the gathering stitch is complete along the length of ribbon, gently gather the ribbon up and, using the attached needle and thread, stitch it into position in the centre of the petals, snaking the gathers until the space is filled with the gathered ribbon. (Do not pull this ribbon up too tightly—it needs to be stitched in several different places to position it realistically, rather than tightly pulled and stitched in the centre of the flower only.)

Leaves: Cut the leaves apart into a pleasing arrangement. Using a complementary coloured thread, stitch them into position, butting them up to the camellia flowers as shown.

Finishing

Frame or mount the completed camellias as desired.

Alternative background

This watercolour wash of the camellia project has been created as a possible background alternative. If desired, copy it to fabric, create the flowers as described above and then simply stitch some vein and outline details on the leaves.

94

CORNFLOWER

This is my favourite photograph. I think I like blue and mauve flowers best of all in the garden. They seem to highlight and act as a foil to the many greens of the garden foliage as well. The photograph was taken outside the Waiheke Island cemetery in the Hauraki Gulf of New Zealand. An unlikely place, but I take opportunities where I find them. The bumblebee was a tad elusive and I had to be patient to ensure it was included in the photograph.

>—+◄►—O—◄►+—◄

Requirements

30 cm (12 in) square hand-dyed cotton fabric, dark tone
    'Moss'
30 cm (12 in) square iron-on interfacing
4 mm silk ribbons:
    1.5 m x colours 20, 21 32, 72, 171
    2 m x colours 23, 102
Rajmahal stranded silk: 29, 113, 115, 421, 521, 805
hand-dyed lace leaves
no. 9 crewel needle for use with silk threads
no. 18 chenille needle for use with silk ribbons
25 cm (10 in) embroidery hoop allows completion of
    work without repositioning

Method

Fuse the interfacing to the back of the cotton fabric. Transfer the design elements required to your fabric (you may need to use the method described for dark fabrics under Pattern Transfer Methods).

The crowded nature of the leaves and grasses at the base of this embroidery mean that you do not have to carefully follow the colours of the green ribbons and threads as used in the photograph.

Background grasses: Work these grasses in 2 strands of Rajmahal 521 and 805, using long straight stitches of different angles and different lengths worked across the base of the design.

flower detail: pistil
stitch, 1 strand
Rajmahal

centre: French
knots, 2 strands
Rajmahal

petals: ribbon stitch,
twisted ribbon stitch,
4 mm silk ribbon

stem: stem stitch,
2 strands Rajmahal

Reed-like grasses: Using the various greens in the 4 mm silk ribbons complete the thicker reed-like grasses and leaves from straight stitch, ribbon stitch and twisted ribbon stitch.

Stems: Worked in stem stitch with 2 strands of Rajmahal 521.

Flowers: These are worked in two different colours of silk ribbon. The flower centres are also worked in two different tones of Rajmahal thread, chosen to match the ribbon and photograph as closely as possible. Work the flower components in the order listed.

Light flowers

Flower centres: 2-wrap French knots, 2 strands Rajmahal 113 (the full flowers have a circular centre, the profile flowers have an oval centre)

Petals: ribbon stitch, twisted ribbon stitch, 4 mm silk ribbon x colour 23

Detail: pistil stitch, 1 strand Rajmahal 113

Dark flowers

Flower centres: 2-wrap French knot, 2 strands Rajmahal 115

Petals: ribbon stitch, twisted ribbon stitch, 4 mm silk ribbon x colour 102

Detail: pistil stitch, 1 strand Rajmahal 115

Leaves: Trim the lace leaves into individual leaves or keep them in clusters. Stitch into place threading some or part of the leaves beneath the strap-like foliage of silk ribbon.

Finishing

Once all the embroidery is complete remove any visible marks from the water-erasable pen by dabbing gently with a cotton bud dipped in water.

Frame or mount as desired.

Watercolour study

This small study based on the major cornflowers embroidery is intended to inspire you to create an individual work. I have provided a watercolour background and diagram, and suggested the stitches you might use, but it is up to you to vary the size, the colours and the diagram as you might wish.

flower centres: 2-wrap French knot,
2 strands Rajmahal; surrounded by
pistil stitch, 1 strand Rajmahal

bud: ribbon stitch, 4 mm silk ribbon
bud calyx (shown shaded): ribbon
stitch, 4 mm silk ribbon

petals: ribbon stitch,
twisted ribbon stitch,
4 mm silk ribbon

stems and leaves: stem stitch,
2 strands Rajmahal

FLANNEL FLOWER

I took this photograph on a bushwalk known as the Flower Bowl Walk, at Point Perpendicular on the mid north coast of New South Wales. Flannel flowers are endemic to where I live as well, and I often take the opportunity in summer to walk among them and photograph them. They are my favourite native flowers with their soft velvety petals and graceful growth habit.

Requirements

30 cm (12 in) square cotton velvet fabric, dark hunter
   green

30 cm (12 in) square iron-on interfacing

4 mm silk ribbons:

3 m x colour 3

1 m x colours 31, 74

Rajmahal stranded art silk: 311, 925

hand-dyed lace leaves/butterfly (not essential but I used
   them to increase the depth of the design by adding
   them to the matt board after mounting)

no. 9 crewel needle for use with silk threads

no. 18 chenille needle for use with silk ribbons

25 cm (10 in) embroidery hoop allows completion of
   work without repositioning

flower centre: 4 mm silk ribbon x colour 31; 1-wrap French knot
flower centre detail/shading: 2 strands Rajmahal 311; French knots

petals: 4 mm silk ribbon x colour 1; bullion detached chain stitch

stem: 2 strands Rajmahal 925; stem stitch

leaves: 4 mm silk ribbon x colour 74; ribbon stitch

Enlarge at 125% on a photocopier

Method

Fuse the interfacing to the back of the cotton velvet fabric. Transfer the design elements required to your fabric (you may need to use the method described for dark fabrics under Pattern Transfer Methods).

Stems: Use 2 strands of Rajmahal 925 and stem stitch.

Centres: The flannel flower centres are created using 4 mm ribbon, colour 31, and a single-wrap French knot.

Petals: Flower petals are worked in bullion detached chain stitch and 4 mm ribbon, colour 1. Angle the tip of each bullion detached chain stitch to give a realistic curve to each petal. The shadowing in the centre of each flower is achieved by working 2-wrap French knots around the perimeter of the green centre using 2 strands Rajmahal 311. Scatter a few of these knots among the silk knots as well.

Spent flower: This flower, at the base of the design, is worked in Rajmahal 311 and simple straight stitches taken back to a central point. Vary the length of these straight stitches slightly.

Buds: Work in 4 mm silk ribbon, colour 1, in bullion detached chain stitch; work the calyx detail on each bud in 2 strands Rajmahal 926 and straight stitch, as indicated in the pattern.

Leaves: Work the leaves in groups of three, in 4 mm silk ribbon, colour 74 and ribbon stitch.

Finishing

Once all the embroidery is complete remove any visible marks from the water-erasable pen by dabbing gently with a cotton bud dipped in water.

Once the design is mounted and framed, you may like to add the hand-dyed lace leaves and butterfly motif to the matt board surrounding the embroidery to enhance the perception of depth in the design.

Watercolour study

This small study based on the major flannel flowers embroidery is intended to inspire you to create an individual work. I have provided a watercolour background and diagram, and suggested the stitches you might use, but it is up to you to vary the size, the colours and the diagram as you might wish.

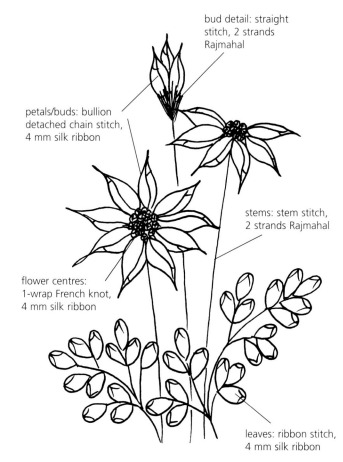

bud detail: straight stitch, 2 strands Rajmahal

petals/buds: bullion detached chain stitch, 4 mm silk ribbon

stems: stem stitch, 2 strands Rajmahal

flower centres: 1-wrap French knot, 4 mm silk ribbon

leaves: ribbon stitch, 4 mm silk ribbon

Roses

Roses are undoubtedly the most popular flower in the world, with hundreds of different types and colours to choose from. I like them all, particularly the old-fashioned, evergreen, repeat-flowering varieties. There are also many and varied ways to embroider a rose. I have used a combination of embroidery stitches and ribbon widths to create four very different roses from just four of the many photographs I have taken over the years (so many, in fact, that my otherwise ever-patient husband now refuses to accompany me when I suggest yet another visit to a rose garden or rose nursery).

Requirements

These materials are sufficient for all four rose embroideries.

4 pieces x 20 cm (8 in) square dupion silk fabric, very soft green

4 pieces x 20 cm (8 in) square iron-on interfacing

4 mm hand-dyed silk ribbon: 0.5 m Colour Streams 'Salt Bush'

7 mm silk ribbons: 2 m x colours 5, 72

7 mm hand-dyed silk ribbons:

    1 m Colour Streams 'Musk Rose'

    2 m Glenlorin 'Jocelyn', 'Rose Gold'

    2 m Colour Streams 'Salt Bush', 'Eucalypt'

13 mm silk hand-dyed silk ribbon: 1 m Colour Streams 'Musk Rose'

Rajmahal stranded art silk: 45, 421, 805

no. 9 crewel needle for use with silk threads

no. 13 chenille needle for use with 13mm silk ribbon.

no. 18 chenille needle for use with 4 and 7 mm silk ribbons

15 cm (6 in) embroidery hoop allows completion of work without repositioning

Old-fashioned species rose
(top right of picture)

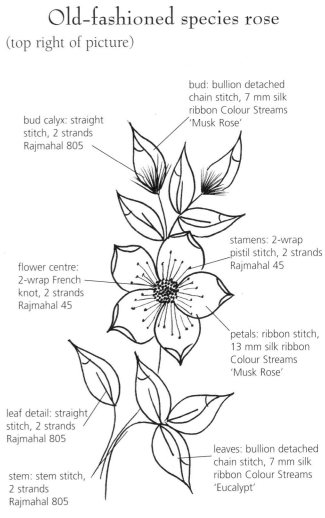

bud: bullion detached chain stitch, 7 mm silk ribbon Colour Streams 'Musk Rose'

bud calyx: straight stitch, 2 strands Rajmahal 805

stamens: 2-wrap pistil stitch, 2 strands Rajmahal 45

flower centre: 2-wrap French knot, 2 strands Rajmahal 45

petals: ribbon stitch, 13 mm silk ribbon Colour Streams 'Musk Rose'

leaf detail: straight stitch, 2 strands Rajmahal 805

leaves: bullion detached chain stitch, 7 mm silk ribbon Colour Streams 'Eucalypt'

stem: stem stitch, 2 strands Rajmahal 805

109

Centifolia rose

(lower right of picture)

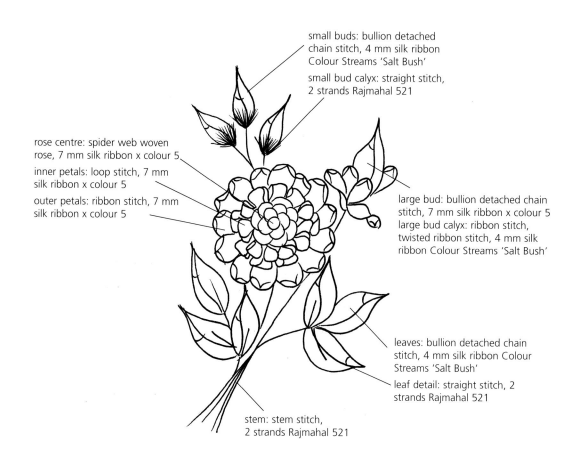

small buds: bullion detached chain stitch, 4 mm silk ribbon Colour Streams 'Salt Bush'

small bud calyx: straight stitch, 2 strands Rajmahal 521

rose centre: spider web woven rose, 7 mm silk ribbon x colour 5

inner petals: loop stitch, 7 mm silk ribbon x colour 5

outer petals: ribbon stitch, 7 mm silk ribbon x colour 5

large bud: bullion detached chain stitch, 7 mm silk ribbon x colour 5

large bud calyx: ribbon stitch, twisted ribbon stitch, 4 mm silk ribbon Colour Streams 'Salt Bush'

leaves: bullion detached chain stitch, 4 mm silk ribbon Colour Streams 'Salt Bush'

leaf detail: straight stitch, 2 strands Rajmahal 521

stem: stem stitch, 2 strands Rajmahal 521

Rugosa rose

(upper left of picture)

outer petals: ribbon stitch, 7 mm silk ribbon Glenlorin 'Rose Gold'

inner petals: ribbon stitch, loop stitch, 7 mm silk ribbon Glenlorin 'Rose Gold'

leaves: bullion detached chain stitch, 7 mm silk ribbon Colour Streams 'Eucalypt'

leaf detail: straight stitch, 2 strands Rajmahal 805

stem: stem stitch, 2 strands Rajmahal 805

Noisette rose

(lower left of picture)

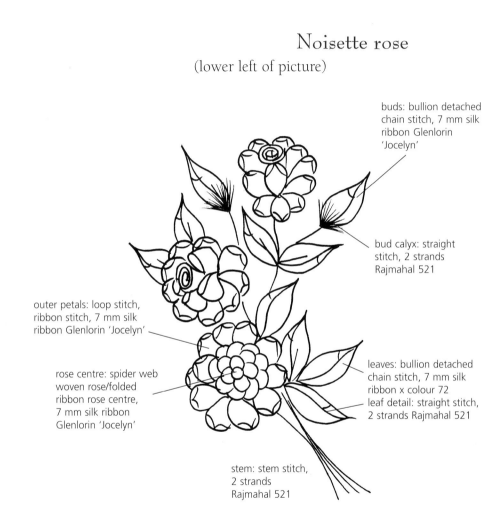

buds: bullion detached chain stitch, 7 mm silk ribbon Glenlorin 'Jocelyn'

bud calyx: straight stitch, 2 strands Rajmahal 521

outer petals: loop stitch, ribbon stitch, 7 mm silk ribbon Glenlorin 'Jocelyn'

rose centre: spider web woven rose/folded ribbon rose centre, 7 mm silk ribbon Glenlorin 'Jocelyn'

leaves: bullion detached chain stitch, 7 mm silk ribbon x colour 72

leaf detail: straight stitch, 2 strands Rajmahal 521

stem: stem stitch, 2 strands Rajmahal 521

Finishing

Once the embroideries are complete remove any visible marks from the water-erasable pen by dabbing gently with a cotton bud dipped in water.

Frame or mount as desired.

Watercolour studies

These watercolours have been produced as possible backgrounds for you to use. You may choose to embroider them in a similar manner to the roses described above or use other stitch combinations to form the flowers.

CRAB-APPLE

Blossom trees are particularly pretty, usually only for a very brief period in early spring. We should always take the time to admire them. These crab-apple flowers were photographed early one morning after light rain, the drops of water still present on the blossom. Against the early morning sky on an otherwise rather dull day it was a memorable sight.

Requirements

30 x 28 cm (12 x 11 in) hand-dyed silk habutae, Colour
    Streams 'Sea Mist'

30 x 28 cm (12 x 11 in) iron-on interfacing

4 mm silk ribbon: 0.5 m x colour 171

7 mm silk ribbon: 2 m Glenlorin 'Annie's Request'

Rajmahal stranded art silk: 44, 45, 311, 421

no. 9 crewel needle for use with silk threads

no. 18 chenille needle for use with silk ribbons

20 cm (8 in) embroidery hoop allows completion of work
    without repositioning

Method

Fuse the interfacing to the back of the silk fabric. Transfer the design elements required to your fabric (see transfer methods)

Complete the stitching using the threads in the order given below.

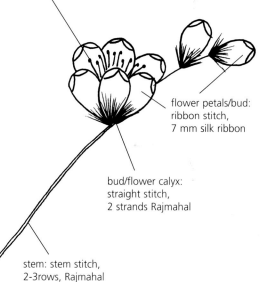

stamens: straight stitch,
1 strand Rajmahal
pollen: 1-wrap French
knot,2 strands Rajmahal

flower petals/bud:
ribbon stitch,
7 mm silk ribbon

bud/flower calyx:
straight stitch,
2 strands Rajmahal

stem: stem stitch,
2-3rows, Rajmahal

116

Stems: stem stitch, 2 strands Rajmahal 311 (if thicker stems are required work 3 rows of stem stitch close together)

Petals/buds: ribbon stitch, 7 mm silk ribbon 'Annie's Request'

Bud calyx: straight stitch, 2 strands Rajmahal 311 and 421

Leaves: bullion detached chain stitch, 4 mm silk ribbon x colour 171

Stamens: straight stitch, 1 strand Rajmahal 44 (these stitches need to be worked before the outer petals formed with 7 mm silk ribbon on the partial flowers)

Pollen: 2-wrap French knot, 2 strands Rajmahal 45

Finishing

Once all the embroidery is complete remove any visible marks from the water-erasable pen by dabbing gently with a cotton bud dipped in water.

Frame or mount as desired.

Watercolour study

This small study based on the major crab-apple embroidery is intended to inspire you to create an individual work. I have provided a watercolour background and diagram, and suggested the stitches you might use, but it is up to you to vary the size, the colours and the diagram as you might wish.

leaves: ribbon stitch, 4 mm or
7 mm silk ribbon depending
of the size of the leaf required

vein detail: stem stitch,
2 strands Rajmahal;

petals: ribbon stitch,
13 mm silk ribbon

bud: ribbon stitch,
4 mm silk ribbon

stems: stem stitch,
2 strands Rajmahal

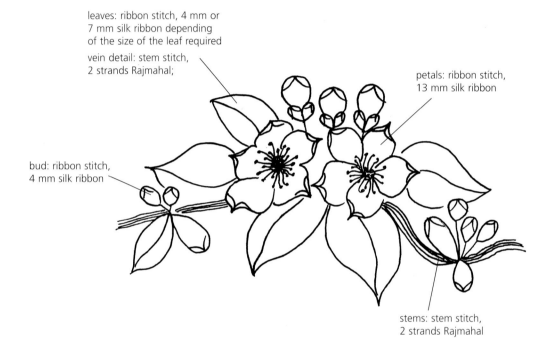

DAISIES

Daisies are such happy flowers and come in many shapes and sizes and a variety of colours. They are also very easy to embroider. These photographs represent not only different sized flowers, from tiny chamomile daisy-like flowers to larger blooms, but also give an idea of colour variations, number of petals, and so on.
In this embroidery it was just too hard to resist substituting barbed wire in place of the strained fencing wire visible in the photograph—such a very Australian icon had to be included in this simple setting.

Requirements

30 x 28 cm (12 x 11 in) hand-dyed silk velvet fabric, Colour Streams 'Salt Bush'

30 x 28 cm (12 x 11 in) iron-on interfacing

2 mm silk ribbon: 1 m x colours 21

4 mm silk ribbons:

   1 m x colours 20, 21, 31, 32, 33, 72, 75, 171

   3 m x colours 1, 72

7 mm silk ribbon:

   1 m x colour 20

   2 m Colour Streams 'Eucalypt'

Rajmahal stranded silk: 29, 45, 221, 521

Rajmahal silver hand-sew thread to create the signature silver web

1 x size 11 black seed bead to create body of spider

no. 9 crewel needle for use with silk threads

no. 18 chenille needle for use with silk ribbons

25 cm (10 in) embroidery hoop allows completion of work without repositioning

Method

Fuse the interfacing to the back of the velvet fabric. Transfer the design elements required to your fabric (you may need to use the method described for dark/thick fabrics under Pattern Transfer Methods).

The crowded nature of the leaves and grasses depicted at the base of this embroidery mean that you do not have to carefully match the colours of the green ribbons and threads used to create them.

Barbed wire: Form twisted cords from 2 strands of Rajmahal 221, stitch these into position, and then create the barbs with 4 straight stitches in a single

strand of the same colour, evenly spaced along the length of 'wire' across the design.

Background grasses: Create these using 2 strands of Rajmahal in colour 521, using long straight stitches worked at different angles and differing lengths across the base of the design. Next, use the length of 2 mm ribbon x colour 21 to create thin grass like stitches across the base of the design, varying the length and the angle of each stitch.

Reed-like grasses: Using the various colours of 4 mm silk ribbons, complete the thicker reed-like grasses and leaves from straight stitch, ribbon stitch and twisted ribbon stitch to create the crowded effect as shown. The 7 mm ribbons are used last, as these thicker grasses appear at the front of the design.

petals: ribbon stitch, twisted ribbon stitch, 4 mm silk ribbon

flower centre: French knots, 4 strands Rajmahal

stem: stem stitch, 2 strands Rajmahal

leaves: straight stitch, 4 mm silk ribbon

Daisy flowers:

Stems: stem stitch, 2 strands Rajmahal 521 (only work the stems where they are visible above the grasses and leaves)

Flower centres: 2-wrap French knot, 4 strands Rajmahal

Petals: ribbon stitch, twisted ribbon stitch, 4 mm silk ribbon x colour 3

Leaves: straight stitch, 4 mm silk ribbon x colour 72

Spider web: The silver web is created by stitching 5 evenly spaced but different length spokes to some chosen point in the design using Rajmahal hand-sew silver thread. Individual straight stitches in silver complete each segment of web. The web stitches never cross the spokes as they will distort them.

The tiny spider is created by sewing the bead into position using Rajmahal 29; angle 4 straight stitches through the bead body to create the legs and stitch the bead body onto the fabric at the same time.

Finishing

Once all the embroidery is complete remove any visible marks from the water-erasable pen by dabbing gently with a cotton bud dipped in water.

Frame or mount as desired.

Enlarge on a photocopier
to 140%

Watercolour study

This small study based on the major daisies embroidery is intended to inspire you to create an individual work. I have provided a watercolour background and diagram, and suggested the stitches you might use, but it is up to you to vary the size, the colours and the diagram as you might wish.

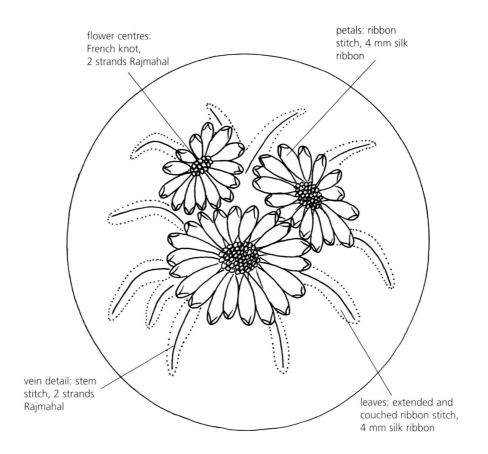

flower centres:
French knot,
2 strands Rajmahal

petals: ribbon
stitch, 4 mm silk
ribbon

vein detail: stem
stitch, 2 strands
Rajmahal

leaves: extended and
couched ribbon stitch,
4 mm silk ribbon

STOCKISTS

Author Helen Dafter supplies, patterns, books and kits for silk ribbon embroidery enthusiasts and for general embroidery requirements. Contact details:

RMB 5430 The Ridgeway
Holgate NSW 2250
Australia
phone: +61 2 4367 7694
email: helen@helendafter.com.au
website: www.helendafter.com.au

The following are manufacturers/distributors only; wholesale enquiries are welcome.

All threads, silk ribbons, needles, etc. are available by mail order from Helen Dafter or from your local specialty embroidery/craft store. If you have difficulty obtaining any requirements I am sure they would be able to provide the closest stockist to you.

Rajmahal (art silk threads)
182 High Street
Kangaroo Flat Victoria 3555
Australia
phone +61 3 5447 7699
email: info@rajmahal.com.au

Glenlorin (hand-dyed silk ribbons)
PO Box 974
Pennant Hills NSW 1715
Australia
phone: +61 2 9980 1993
email: glenlorin@optusnet.com.au

Colour Streams (hand-dyed silk ribbons)
5 Palm Avenue
Mullumbimby NSW 2482
Australia
phone: +61 2 6684 2577
email: colourstreams@ozemail.com.au